Meditations for Miserable People
(Who want to stay that way)

Dan Goodman

ST. MARTIN'S PAPERBACKS

MEDITATIONS FOR MISERABLE PEOPLE (WHO REALLY WANT TO STAY THAT WAY)

Copyright © 1995 by Dan Goodman.

ISBN: 0-312-95514-6

Printed in the United States of America

St. Martin's Paperbacks trade paperback edition / July 1995

10 9 8 7 6 5 4 3 2 1

To my parents, Les and Joyce, who I can never make as miserable as they sometimes make each other. You guys are the best.

To my sister, Debbie, who never made me as miserable as I'm sure I made her.

To all my friends . . . or at least the people who say they're my friends.

And, of course, to all the girls who dumped me thinking I would never amount to anything. I hope this book makes you as miserable as you all made me.

—D.G.

Hope is like the sun,
which, as I journey toward it,
is bound to give me cancer.

∞

When God shuts a door,
He opens a window—then pisses out
of it onto my life.

Self-discovery is useless unless I
discover I'm somebody else.

∞

I am not an unattractive person.
I am downright hideous.

∞

If I fall off the wagon
no one will know because
I have no friends.

To bring harmony into
my relationships with others
I must first realize that their lives
are much better than mine.

Knowing and understanding myself
helps me realize just how worthless
I really am.

∞

If I'm impatient with the pace of my
recovery, I should go ahead and kill
myself.

∞

Life is a series of valleys and more
valleys, of which I will fall into
every single one.

I deserve true love—even if
it costs me $3.99 a minute.

∞

People may disappoint me
but not nearly as much as I
will disappoint myself.

God never listens.
In fact, He hates my guts.

∞

The starting point for misery is
believing I deserve every ounce of it.

∞

There is nothing wrong with crying
when your life is as pitiful as mine.

If I let go of the feelings
which cause me pain,
I would have no feelings at all.

∞

Happiness doesn't come from having
what you want . . . in fact, it doesn't
come from anything at all.

∞

If I rely on what I can do
I will not go far.

Loneliness is a harbor in which I will drown every day of my miserable existence.

∞

I have low self-esteem, but that's only because I am worthless.

∞

Whatever I leave to God He will not do, for He, like everybody else, hates me with a passion.

In helping others you're wasting your time because they're just calling you a loser behind your back.

∞

I forsake lasting recovery because I know I am not capable of attaining anything.

∞

Criticize, don't analyze.

The first step in finding God is
accepting His presence and the fact
that He's just ignoring you.

∞

The rewards of tolerance
on a personal level are
misery, abuse, and eventual death.

If you are honest with yourself,
loneliness and despair are easily
within reach.

∞

A new day can begin to suck at any
time . . . like right now, for instance.

∞

I cannot retrieve my inner child,
for it is dead and buried
in my backyard.

When I eliminate the impossible,
whatever remains is still not attainable
by someone like me.

∞

When you feel unloved, get used to it,
because you know it's the truth.

∞

I should accept the flaws in my
character, for without them
I would have no character at all.

God forgives all people,
but He still holds a grudge against me.

∞

Listening open-mindedly to others is a
waste of time because people don't like
me and want me to fail.

God will be a positive force in my life,
then kill me in some grotesque
fashion.

∞

Live in the here and now,
for tomorrow is sure to be
just as miserable.

All of my relationships would be
stronger if I was simply not
part of them.

∞

The mistakes I make today
I will make again tomorrow
because I am stupid and slow.

∞

If at first you don't succeed, give up.

I cannot do everything by myself,
no matter how often people ask me
to try.

∞

Life is best measured
one miserable failure at a time.

∞

When I realize what I have to be
thankful for, it is only then that I
realize how worthless my life really is.

I cannot achieve complete humility—
although complete humiliation is
always within reach.

By reminding myself of the past
I remind myself that I'm still
the same loser I've always been.

∞

I will not put off till tomorrow
what I can fail at today.

∞

Saying "good-bye" is always painful,
except for the people who are saying it
to me.

Self-realization comes not from
believing you are a loser,
but by knowing it.

∞

Believing in myself is easy
when I believe I will fail.

∞

Closing my eyes to the imbecile I am
doesn't erase the memories of
the imbecile I was.

If I am patient with myself
it will only take me longer to realize
I am feeble.

∞

Dependency isn't a problem unless
I'm depending on myself.

∞

I am not afraid of failure.
In fact, I'm getting used to it.

The only decision I will ever regret is
the last one that I made.

∞

I am not inferior to other people.
I am inferior to all people.

It is not that I have nothing to give,
but rather that no one wants
what I have.

∞

In learning to accept myself I learn to
accept the worst that life has to offer.

∞

Writing a "personal inventory" is easy
when you have nothing to show for
your life.

My faith in a Higher Power can help
me succeed . . . but it won't . . . and
I will fail.

∞

The best way I can help other people is
to leave them alone.

∞

I know that life will one day get better,
and that one day will be the day
that I die.

Running away accomplishes nothing, but for me accomplishing nothing is nothing new.

My feelings are not facts unless
I feel that I'm an idiot.

∞

I do not fear my life coming to an
end, but others fear that end may not
come soon enough.

∞

When I really put my mind to it,
anything is impossible.

Life will change day by day,
and it will always change for the worse.

∞

I will not deny myself feelings of
pleasure when there are so many
others who wish to do it for me.

∞

Jealousy is wanting what others have.
Stupidity is thinking you might
one day get it.

A competitive relationship will always have a loser, just like any relationship with me.

∞

If I don't try something for fear of looking bad I must remember that I look bad anyway.

God has a plan for you and
it's that you will fail miserably at
everything you do.

∞

Today I will focus on my defects
because defects are all I have.

∞

I will not live up to others'
expectations unless, of course,
they expect me to fail.

∞

Every man has a rainy corner in
his life and my rain has spread to
the whole damn room.

Everyone brings something to a
relationship and to my relationships
I always bring the end.

∞

If I have a negative picture of myself
I must realize that the camera
doesn't lie.

Accepting your limitations makes you humble. The limitations themselves make you an idiot.

∞

I have no "significant other" because I myself am insignificant.

∞

Beauty is in the eye of the beholder as long as the beholder isn't looking at me.

∞

Today I will be giving and kind
and it won't make a difference
as I am both hated and ignored.

∞

Life doesn't have to be
depressing and miserable . . .
but it is, so get used to it.

If you don't like who you are
you're not alone. No one else
likes who you are, either.

∞

Self-restraint is not important
because nobody really cares
what I do or say.

•33•

When times get tough, quit.
No one will care.

∞

What you achieve is not important
when you can't achieve anything.

∞

By writing my fears down on paper
I will see that not only am I afraid of
everything but that I also have
really bad penmanship.

Sharing myself with another person is
the quickest way to get that person to
loathe me.

∞

Every person's journey through life is
unique and mine is uniquely boring
and depressing.

∞

I am not the problem.
I am not the solution.
I am nothing, and everyone knows it.

My behavior today will not be
self-defeating as I am more easily
defeated by others.

∞

Today I will make the best of a bad
situation, which is basically
every situation I have.

∞

The answers to your questions are
right within you, and that is why
your answers will always be wrong.

•36•

Anyone can be successful
if their goal in life is to be
better than me.

∞

Once I learn to forgive,
my heart will be open to further
pain and misery.

Life won't get me down today
because I'm already down and
I plan on staying there.

∞

I will not believe everything I hear
unless I hear that nobody likes me.

∞

It is not easy to make friends,
but for me it's easy to make
friends sick.

The way to avoid setting unrealistic
goals is to avoid setting goals
in the first place.

∞

Once you fear failure you fear the
only thing you'll probably ever know.

∞

Life isn't over when we die . . .
it's pretty much over right now.

The key to happiness has been
duplicated and given to everyone else
but me.

∞

Always strive to do your worst since
your worst is basically all you can do.

∞

God didn't give me the power to
reason and that's but one reason why
I have no power.

I will try to fulfill the demands of
others since they only demand that
I leave them alone.

∞

Everyone faces adversity
the moment they face me.

∞

True love comes but once in a lifetime
as long as the lifetime isn't my own.

What I do after a mistake isn't really
important since I already screwed up
like a big fat jerk.

∞

Today I will find a sense of belonging
and I will sense that I belong
alone and depressed.

Good things don't happen by
coincidence, they just don't happen.

∞

God helps those who help themselves
if they help themselves to hurting me.

Today I will start on my road to recovery and tonight I will discover it was just a dead end.

∞

The breeze of divine grace is blowing upon me, covering my life with germs and disease.

∞

Today I will not reach out to others since nobody really wants me to touch them.

•44•

Setbacks and failures are not
a part of my life, they *are* my life.

∞

I no longer need to compromise my
dignity because worthless people
like me have no dignity.

∞

Something good comes out of
everything, unless it was something
done by me.

"Getting away" won't solve your problems, but it'll sure make everyone around you a lot happier.

∞

If I think before I act, it will only take me longer to make the wrong decision.

∞

Don't be afraid to be yourself, because no one pays much attention to you anyway.

Looking back at where I came from
only proves that I haven't come far.

∞

Opportunity is nothing more than
discovering a new way to fail.

∞

Self-pity never accomplishes anything,
but then again, neither do I.

Today I will learn to accept the love of
others, which shouldn't take long,
since nobody loves me.

∞

One day the meek shall inherit the
Earth . . . then they too will beat
the crap out of me.

If I enjoy what I do
I must be doing something wrong.

∞

Love is two people finding each other
and being thankful that they
didn't find me.

∞

When I compare myself with others
I will not come up short because
I won't come up at all.

Life has so much to offer,
but it will only offer it to other people.

∞

Blaming others is never right,
unless the other being blamed is me.

∞

It's not important what people think of
me because I'm not that important
to begin with.

If I trust in what I know I will be
forced to trust in nothing.

∞

Life is nothing but a series of changes
bringing misery, pain and
a hideous death.

By channeling my ideas into
constructive action I will realize
how stupid my ideas really are.

The more I let other people run my
life the better off I know I will be.

∞

People won't love you for what you are
. . . they simply won't love you.

∞

Everyone has hopes in life and
most people hope that
I leave them alone.

I will not suffer needlessly today,
but I will suffer because I need to.

∞

Things will turn out the way they're
supposed to, but only when they're
supposed to turn out bad.

∞

You cannot be satisfied with what you
have, since everyone knows you have
absolutely nothing.

•54•

Every experience can be a positive one
as long as I am not a part of it.

∞

Everyone wants something from me,
and they all want me to
stay the hell away.

∞

I can't be all things to all people . . .
unless they're all bad things.

It is better to have loved and lost,
especially for those who might have
loved me.

Self-pity isn't something I'm proud of,
but I have nothing to be proud of
anyway.

∞

I will not be alone in suffering,
but I will be alone because
I am insufferable.

∞

The man who feels good about himself
is the man who realizes he could have
been me.

Don't get people to talk about
their problems unless you want to
hear them talk about you.

∞

Be rotten to yourself today.
You deserve it.

∞

The more I give of myself to others
the more I realize there wasn't much
of me to begin with.

Yesterday's regrets and tomorrow's
anxieties will not detract from
the misery of today.

∞

I can be what I want and do what
I want if I want to be an idiot and
do absolutely nothing.

Everyone makes mistakes,
especially the people who think
I have a life.

∞

If you focus on what's really important
you'll never have to focus on yourself.

∞

Today I will believe in God,
and as usual He won't believe in me.

My relationships with others will not
be give-and-take but
give-and-take off.

∞

Accepting others as they are means
accepting that they are better than me.

∞

God can touch me like no person
because no person really wants to
touch me.

As long as I do the best I can
I'm certain to fail at everything I do.

∞

Never underestimate yourself
when others are happy to do it for you.

Today I will find out where I stand in
the world, and wherever it is,
I will stand there alone.

∞

The best things in life are the things
that belong to everyone but me.

∞

I can learn to be my own best friend,
but then I remember that I
don't really like me.

People will never give up on me
because they never believed in me
to begin with.

∞

I will not regret what happened
yesterday as much as I regret
what happens today.

•64•

I am not alone in this world,
I'm simply being ignored by
every living being.

∞

If I never try I'll never find out
what else I could have failed at.

∞

By raising my self-awareness I will
soon be aware that nobody likes me.

If I lie to myself it's only because
no one else will listen to what I say.

∞

Things are not always what they
appear to be unless they appear to be
hopeless and futile.

∞

Today I will remember that things will
always work out for the worst.

Misery loves company,
unless that company is me.

∞

Painful feelings don't last forever.
They're simply replaced by
even more painful feelings.

∞

I do not need the approval of others,
which is lucky for me,
since I know I'll never get it.

True beauty resides in the heart.
True ugliness resides in my face.

∞

It isn't important what people think of
me, it's just plain sad.

∞

Every great act begins with an idea,
and every bad act begins with
an idea from me.

Paying attention to the good things in life takes no time at all when you have no good things to pay attention to . . . and you don't.

Today may seem the same as yesterday,
but in reality it's worse.

∞

When people truly listen to what I say,
they will realize what a mistake that
was and go back to ignoring me.

∞

Any goal is realistic as long as I realize
I'll never attain it.

God isn't saving the best for last,
He's saving it for somebody
other than you.

Today I will not set myself up to fail.
The failure will come naturally
as it always does.

∞

Just when I think I've become
unimportant I realize, well,
I've always been unimportant.

∞

The best relationships are those which
have nothing to do with me.

God gives me only what I can handle,
which is why God gives me
nothing at all.

∞

Today I will internalize the problems
of others since their problems are
basically a result of knowing me.

I will not subject myself to a solid relationship. I deserve worse.

∞

If I blame myself for every little problem it is only because every problem is my fault.

∞

Happiness is inside everybody who isn't around me.

People don't hate what I stand for,
they hate that I stand near them.

∞

Whatever happens life goes on,
and it will continue to rot and
bring me great pain.

By reaching out to another
I'll find yet another person that wants
nothing to do with me.

∞

It's not true that you can't please
everybody. The truth is that you can't
please anybody.

•76•

No one loves me until I love myself.
And even then no one will love me.

∞

The ending of one failure is nothing
more than the beginning of another.

∞

One person can make a difference
unless the person in question is me.

Some things are better left unsaid,
such as anything that would have been
said by me.

∞

Inside every problem lie the seeds to
even more problems of which I will
find every single one.

∞

I can easily avoid confrontation
because everyone ignores me.

Live each day as if it was your last,
because everyone is hoping that it is.

Ask and ye shall not receive,
for God hates ye.

∞

A job worth doing is a job worth
giving to someone other than me.

∞

Expect the worst, you'll get the worst.
Expect the best, you'll still get the
worst.

Winning isn't everything,
it's just something else that never
happens to me.

∞

Hope is everywhere that I'm not.

∞

I control my own destiny and
that's why I'm destined for misery
and doom.

Friends don't let friends
be friends with me.

∞

Everyone has a special talent,
and mine is having no talents at all.

∞

I am the best person I can be,
which is pretty lame.

Today God will answer your prayers,
and the answer will be "NO!"

∞

Having hope is a decision.
Having no hope is a reality.

My life is out of my hands,
and knowing me, that's probably
for the best.

∞

Life is not a competition,
it's simply one big loss after another.

∞

If I do not think of myself as a loser,
then I'm obviously not thinking
very hard.

Today I will live to the best of my
abilities, until I remember that I have
no abilities.

∞

Nothing in life happens instantly,
except for people's disliking of me.

∞

I am not a bad person getting good,
but a miserable person getting
nowhere.

God wants the best for everyone,
and that's why he's keeping them all
away from me.

Good friends make bad lovers and
no friends make . . . me.

∞

The difference between hearing and
listening is not important since
nobody wants to talk to me anyway.

∞

Some things in life were not meant to
be, and something tells me that
I am one of them.

He who insists on rehashing the past
will miss the despair and misery
of today.

∞

When I finally concede to my
innermost self it is then that I
concede I really am a loser.

Today my life will be an open book
that no one in their right mind
will want to read.

∞

Fear does not cause sorrow and regret
. . . I do.

∞

Communicate with God through
meditation and he will tell you to
shut up like everyone else does.

True love isn't blind,
it just doesn't want to meet
someone like you.

I have to live my life for me,
although I'm sure someone else
could do a much better job.

∞

Being willing to ask for help is the
first step in realizing that no one
wants to help a loser like you.

I do not know what the future holds
for me, but I know it's gonna hurt . . .
and it's gonna hurt bad.

You should not fear life, because you
have no life in the first place.

∞

I do not care what others think of me
because I know that they don't think
of me at all.

∞

I am not afraid to make mistakes,
for without them I wouldn't make
anything at all.

•93•

Do unto others and they won't do unto
you because everything you do
is stupid.

∞

If I look at my problems with a fresh
perspective I will see that they're
worse than I originally thought.

∞

Happiness is seeing someone you love
. . . until they see you and
close the blinds.

Nobody has all the answers.
In fact, I don't have any.

∞

No one can treat me as bad as I treat
myself, although everyone
deserves to try.

∞

Remember the way things used to be
and realize that life is only
getting worse.

A day without love is a day like
every other day I've lived so far.

∞

God has His own agenda . . .
and I'm not on it.

The most difficult experiences in life
are those which unfortunately were
experienced with me.

∞

I have nothing to fall back on because
there's nowhere to fall from the
bottom.

∞

My way isn't always the right way.
In fact, it's never the right way.

Accentuate the negative,
because you know it's all you have.

Boredom is a state of mind that will
only disappear when I do.

∞

Stepping stones are merely
stumbling blocks in disguise.

∞

The more I listen to myself,
the more I realize why people
ignore me.

I will not lose control today
for I never had any control
to begin with.

∞

It's not what you do but how you do it,
and you're gonna do it very badly.

∞

No two men are created equal,
which is a damn good thing for
everybody else.

•100•

You shouldn't run away from your problems, you should simply run away.

∞

If no one approves of what you're doing, then you're probably doing what you always do.

∞

Today I will take nothing for granted, since I know I'm not gonna get anything anyway.

Every person is a piece of God's plan,
and I am the piece that simply
doesn't fit.

∞

I am not undeserving of love,
I am simply undeserving of everything.

∞

Never be ashamed of failure,
just be ashamed of yourself.

People won't hurt you for the wrong reason, they'll hurt you for any reason they want.

∞

True friends will never desert you, because you have no true friends in the first place.

God grant me the serenity to accept
the things I cannot change, the
courage to change the things I can,
and the wisdom to know that I really
can't do either.